Stolen Lives

D1409189

Ahmed A. Miqdad

Editor: Jasmine Choudhury

2015

Cover Image Courtesy of Irina Naji

Dedication

I would like to dedicate this poetry book to Palestine, the souls of martyrs, the Wounds, and the Palestinian prisoners inside the Israeli jails.

CONTENTS

PREFACE

Palestine has been living since many years under the Israeli occupation. Since that time, each day is considered as a new story of suffering, killing, violation, and pain to the Palestinians. As soon as they finish from a crisis, another one starts emerging and drawing a new challenge in front of them. The Palestinian cause has begun when the Israeli army occupied the Palestinian lands and obliged the Palestinians to leave their homes and villages under the threat of killing and terrorism. Then, the Israeli occupation lasts till nowadays.

The Israelis used all kinds and means to remove the Palestinian cause from the scene but the Palestinians do all their best to face the occupation by all simple means they own.

By all these endeavors, the Palestinian cause becomes like a natural phenomenon which all free people recognized as "an occupied country". People start all over the world moving and condemning the Israeli occupation and the crimes, slaughters, and destruction which are committed by the occupation. Supporters use all their available facilities to make the Palestinian cause more clear and public. They use the social media to get the true news and reports about Palestine and what is going on there. The activists make the Palestine issue on the top of their priority and they start publishing photos, news and live videos from Palestine to show the people around the world the real image which is hidden from them by the western media. For example, they demonstrate in the western capitals and cities in order to awake the people and spread knowledge about Palestine. During the last years, the numbers of pro-Palestine people are getting bigger and wider. Many of the supporters and activists are film-makers, poets, writers, actors, and journalists. They used all their possibilities to raise the awareness of people and increasing the supporters of the Palestinian cause.

One of the most effective weapons that play a major role in serving the Palestinian cause is literature. There are many authors and writers write about history, people, culture, catastrophes, and suffering of the Palestinian under the Israeli occupation. This helps in spreading the truth about Palestine and making more people stay beside the Palestinian in their resistance against the occupation. Many writers write novels, drama, poetry and short stories to describe the hard life of Palestinians and how the Israeli occupation treat them less than animals without any right of freedom and humanity. All these kinds of literature come up from the witnessed experiences of the authors who live and taste the pain and suffering themselves.

Poetry plays a very significant and important role of spreading not only knowledge but also emotions and feelings of the poets to the readers and this put a noticeable impact on the readers because they don't read only words but they feel the emotions and feelings of the poet which affect him to translate his feelings into words then poems. It is so clear that poetry can portray a very clear image of describing an event with feelings and this will make the reader reacting with the event definitely.

The poet writes his words from the live experiences on an event that he witnessed by his eyes or heart. Then, the poet tries to put experiences into words which are filled of feelings to attract the intention of readers and make them live the good and bad experiences and experiments that the poet has been living during different instances. Moreover, the poet can provoke people to go out and fight against the injustice and occupation.

I am as a Palestinian poet who has lived under the Israeli occupation since my birth. I have witnessed countless and unlimited crimes against the Palestinians and I have lived more than three brutal wars on Gaza during the last ten years.

I am the poet who has been living under the unfair Israeli siege on Gaza since years till now. I am that poet who has been watching the pain and suffering of my people. I am that poet, who saw the tears of mothers and fathers, the shouting of orphans and widows, watching the homeless inside the schools, and looking at martyrs and wounds in the hospitals. All this affects and makes me a poet who aims to deliver the real image and truth to people who haven't heard about Palestine. I aim to transfer my feelings and emotions into poems to describe the life of the Palestinians and I intend to illustrate the brutality of the Israeli' occupation.

I wish that my poems will be able to show the readers the real images about the hard life, suffering and pain of the Palestine and I hope my poems help to attract more supporters to Palestinian cause. I hope that I was successful in writing more poems to demonstrate and illustrate Palestine clearly to western people. Please, don't hesitate to pass the word and tell your friends and family about Palestine and recommend my books to them.

1 - I MISS MY BED

I miss my bed,
and the heavy pink blanket,
there in that room,
in my ruined home.
They destroyed it without reason.
A phone call from a man
asked us to leave the home.
No time to think,
no time to grab my precious things,
it was enough to save our souls.
Standing away,
in the narrow road,
looking sadly up at my beautiful home,
just waiting for a rocket to destroy it all.
Moments... that felt like forever,
the rockets rained down,
the shrapnel flew.
There as the ashes cover the scene,
I stand with my family in the cold darkness.
Kind neighbors showed solidarity,
coming out to cover our shivering bodies,
during this endless night.

I miss the warmth,
of my beautiful room,
Where I once hung sky blue curtains,

they destroyed it all,
only for my family to now join
our ever growing neighbors in tents.
Burning wood to get warm,
our broken bodies shake.
We cook on the fire in open skies,
just to survive.
Unable to sleep as we have,
rats for our neighbors.
In the distance I hear dogs barking,
I'm so afraid of the night.
The tattered homes
are like the night ghosts.
The winds whistle,
through the rubble.
Dreams are full with shredded bodies,
like a nightmare.
I'm screaming and I cry for the children,
I see near the pavement.
They're asking for help,
as they close their eyes one last time,
as they pass away.

I miss my bed,
and warm cozy nights.
So comfortable they were,
without my fear of nightmares.
Now the rough feeling covers
they hurt my little body in
the cold winter haze,
turn my fingers blue,
as the cold air breezes through my hair.
But most of all I think
I miss humanity,
more than my warm cozy bed.

2 – WINGLESS GAZA

They cut your wings,
broke your weak feet.
Put you in a cage, and closed its doors.
They left you alone,
inside a prison.
You can't feed your children,
or heal your wounds,
even though you have your wings,
your wings sound useless.
They want to feed you,
like caged birds.
They will give you food,
according to their mood.
They want to pour water,
just enough to keep you alive.
The birds will sometimes
wash its feathers with some of water,
for it has more faith
than these who called humans.
The birds don't care about tomorrow,
they enjoy today,
and tomorrow will have its own story.

Oh Gaza, like the birds,
while the world conspire against you,
puts you inside this open cage.

They broke your wings,
with the attacks against you,
they left you fatigued.
But your wings will grow once more I believe,
their bits of food and water,
Will be needed no more.
For those who have dignity,
don't forget also have God
A God who can feed a blind snake,
with a generous hunt.

Gaza, who's trust in God,
can never be broken.
You will fly once again,
with the grace of the almighty.

3 – I CAN'T BREATHE

I can't breathe,
I am a Palestinian.
They occupied my land,
and burned me out.
They cut my olive trees
and stole out blessings.

I can't breathe,
I am a Palestinian.
They built their wall
on our given lands.
Destroyed the farms,
and bulldozed our homes.
They separated our families,
so even a mother can't reach
her daughter
on the other side.
They deprive us
from reaching our lands.

I can't breathe,
I am a Palestinian.
They kill us daily,
lock up our children,
confiscate our lands,
steal our properties.

They blow up our homes,
and make thousands of us homeless.
They tear our children's bodies,
with their parts under the rubble.

I can't breathe,
I am a Palestinian.
I have the right to resist.
To fight for my rights,
to defend my ancestral land,
and to protect my home.
To smell the fresh air,
and drink the pure water.
I have the right
to demonstrate against their wall
that is a symbol of apartheid,

I can't breathe,
I am a Palestinian,
who has dignity above all,
I will never give up,
in spite of your torture.
You shoot your gas grenades,
to keep me back.
To stop my legal demonstration
that's your dream.
But it can never be real.

I can't breathe,
You kill me with gas.
You grab my throat
with your bloody hands.
You let my soul fly,
and then............
my body is sacrificed,
for the sake of my homeland,
you killed me.
But the story will not end there,
because we will never give up.
We are too hard to be broken.

4 – WHAT ARE YOU WAITING FOR?

What are you waiting for?,
We have lost our land,
forced to leave our homes.
We live as refugees,
waiting for our return,
to our ancestor's land,
we are killed every day,
and will you just watch?.

What are you waiting for?,
They destroyed our homes,
and eradicated our roots.
Thousands of martyrs,
dying for the sake of Palestine.
All of us are wounded,
hundreds of thousands of bodies,
and the rest walk by with hearts ablaze,
homeless and crowded,
but the world still tells us,
it's all unfounded.

What are you waiting for?,
Children are dying,
in the embrace of their parents,
and orphans are awaiting mercy,
from this neglectful world

Innocents are killed savagely,
still waiting for human rights to move.
But it seems that,
we are not humans,
maybe we are not.
As Palestinians it seems are a miracle.
We will never be beaten,
like the miracles of bygone prophets,
so clear like the sun,
in a pure blue sky.

What are you waiting for?,
While the siege is threatening our souls,
and our children are dying,
at the gates of our brothers.
They have no mercy,
They smile in the face of our deaths.
They keep us in a prison,
surrounded by our enemies,
who pretend to be friends.

What are you waiting for?,
Palestine is bleeding,
and Gaza is dying.
If you don't move now,
When will you move?!!!,
What are you waiting for?

5 – HELL ON EARTH FOR GAZA

Have you ever felt hell on earth?,
Is it a strange question?
We all know that hell exists,
but how is it a hell on earth?,
Well, it is a hell on earth,
while you live in your paradise,
others are in hell.
When the dark night,
becomes light as the day.
The military torches are lit
high above in the sky.
The noisy sounds of killer planes,
hover over our heads.

The hell is on earth for Gaza,
when the bombs kill innocent children,
turning little bodies to ash.
The huge bombs attack Gaza,
which destroyed our homes,
and kill parents and children alike.

The hell is on earth for Gaza,
when the terrified leave their homes,
and reside in the schools.
They leave all their properties,

escaping barely with their lives.
Neighbors give them food and water.
They await on others to give them shelter,

The hell is on earth for Gaza,
when you are unable
to protect your family,
from the intense bombing
that aim to destroy us all.
The children are afraid,
they are crying and screaming,
holding on to you for dear life.
They think you have
the power to protect them,
But they don't know,
you will die before them,
while trying, and protecting
their innocent lives.

The hell is on earth for Gaza,
when the beds in the hospital are filled,
and the wounded are forced to lay on the ground.
They plead for more blood,
it seems the donations are not enough,
to save lives of the wounded,
as they also start to attack
the hospitals and clinics.
The innocent die,
While in treatment.

The hell is on earth for Gaza,
when the family is at home,
and suddenly one of your children gets injured.
The ambulance is unable to reach him on time,
you have a feeling it won't make it,
due to heavy shelling outside.
You look at your son,
while he is bleeding,
and you are helpless,
as you witness him,
take his last breath.

The hell is on earth for Gaza,

when thousands of tons of weapons,
fall down in a small and crowded area,
under continuous siege.
Yet the world watches on in silence,
while Gaza is burning and people are dying.
Your silence doesn't help good people,
for the creators of hell
are the ones that are silent.

6 – WELCOME TO DEATH

Some say, "Life is beautiful,
it is full of happiness and joy,
and your children will
complete the beauty in life.
A kind wife
will make life more sweet,
especially if you have a luxurious house.
You are able to create your own happiness,
as a kid I thought "yes it's the truth",
but the reality was not like that.

They were all liars.
I want to ask them all,
how can you create happiness,
for a man who has lost everything
that is beautiful in this life????

Who lost his lovely children,
and watched them die in his sight,
he was burning,
and was unable to move,
to rescue his children.

Who lost his precious wife,
during the last bombardment,
while she's preparing food
to feed the frightened children.

They were waiting for their food,
in a dimly lit shelter,
and playing with candles,
but missiles don't differentiate,
between the guilty or the innocent.

Who lost his mother,
in her warm bed,
while she was sleeping,
under the window.
I found her sinking in her own blood,
her head on the pillow.
As she took my hand,
she said to me "son, take care of your family",
but she didn't know
they proceeded her to heaven,
and they left me alone.

Take all my money,
and all that I own,
but let me see my family again.
Let me kiss my children one last time.
I have nothing to lose,
I welcome death.
For it maybe better,
from your beautiful life,
at least I will be with them
Once again.

7 – GET ANGRY

Get angry,
if you are human,
get angry.
When you see
your neighbors have no food,
or forced from their homes.
While your country
is paying trillions for others,
by sending ships of weapons.
these weapons,
they kill the innocents in Palestine.

Get angry,
when you feel
humanity is being killed,
and deceived with their,
fake and illegal justifications.

Get angry,
when they hide the truth,
through their controlled media,
while showing you the opposite image.
They make the murderers
a hero defending humanity,
and giving out Noble Prizes,
while the victim is dying,

and aching from pain.

Get angry,
when you see,
innocent children being shredded,
With your tax money.
The orphans lost their parents,
because of your government's support.

Get angry,
when you hear,
the voices of the voiceless,
who are burning,
and buried under the rubble,
by the Israeli bombs.

Get angry,
when you see,
complete families erased,
from the civil records,
and deprive them,
from their natural lives as humans.

Get angry,
when you feel,
the parents are so scared,
and the children are crying,
they don't have anything,
to protect them from the monsters,
who claim mercy and democracy.

Get angry,
when you hear about terrorism,
and who fights against it,
because the ones who fight,
are the ones who create it.
To achieve some purpose,
we look to the surface,
and neglect the bottom,
although it holds many of the secrets.

Get angry,
if you see,

Homes destroyed,
the children ripped apart,
the widowed women,
the poor people,
get angry,
if you are human.

8 – THE KIDNAPPED HAPPINESS

I count the days to pass,
and prepare myself,
for the best day of my life.
It is not just for me,
but also for my proud parents.
How I love to see them smile.

I invited my friends and relatives,
to share my wedding day.
I prepared my immaculate suit to wear
and hope my bride is ready,
with her glossy white dress.
It will be so romantic.

Just a week 'til the big day.
I ask God to make it
pass without any delay.
But the choice of my destiny was already planned,
the attacks started on Gaza without mercy.
Hundreds were wounded and martyred.
All I hear are bombs and screaming wherever I turn,
demolished homes and homeless people.
we cancel all our celebrations,
and make it a silent marriage with God.
The enemy would not allow
for any more than that.

They started their land incursions.
My home's near the borders,
they demolished it without mercy.
Our future bedroom all but disappeared,
and my once immaculate suit?
now just so torn without recognition.
My life's work under heaps of rocks.

I will start my life over,
a promise to myself.
I WILL celebrate our union
even without a home.
We shall celebrate our marriage,
in a school classroom.
I pray we have lots of children,
to defend this assault and occupation.

The aggressors thought
they would conquer my will.
I will never allow them
to destroy my happiness while I
still have breath in my body.
I will overcome their cruel plan,
again and again 'til my last breath.

9 – WHERE IS IT?

Where is it?,
"I don't know the location,
I have never heard of it"
people say to me,
when I say " I am from Palestine".

I was sure they would know
of our talented singers,
and the names of our famous belly dancers.
But they don't know my precious Palestine.
I want to ask,
have you read my history,
or have you studied geography.
But it seems that there's a failure,
In your schools.

If I asked you,
" Do you know Israel?"
you will usually say " Yes"
I reply to you
I'll tell you a TRUTH you don't often hear,
" We are occupied by Israel".

forgive me
for calling your education a failure,
because it's not your fault,

and Palestine is small
to see it on a map.
They deceived you
when they taught you.
Israel is located between Africa and Asia.
They manipulated the real history,
when they neglected Palestine,
and hid the existence of the Israeli state.

Don't you listen to international news?
or maybe you're just interested
in drinking and dancing,
maybe stories of lust probably attracts you
more than a thousand killed in Palestine.
Is this the planet you prefer to belong to?
Or is this the planet that you have created for yourself?
Palestine has been suffering for decades and decades,
and still even now..............
every day of the year,
It has its own story.
The massacres and genocide
against the nation of Palestine.
Are all these blood drenched years
not enough for you yet
to know the reality of a once beautiful
PALESTINE?.

The last aggression on my people
lasted fifty-one days.
Targeted explosions at civilians,
where thousands of children died.
tens of thousands were wounded,
hundreds of thousands made homeless
without mercy.
But will any of this matter or move you,
when you have the FREEDOM
to drink and to dance?

I know you are deceived,
and we do not blame you.
Your media hides the truth
and reality is evaded.
News and documentary programs

Heavily distorted.
This is not the media's job,
but they are monitored,
they give you a version that tells you,
only about Palestine
launching rockets on Israel.
They tell you we love violence,
and that Israelis are injured,
and in constant fear.
But what they leave out and pretend
isn't happening, Is in fact.....
Israel killed over two thousands Palestinians,
and left orphans, widows and childless mothers
in their savage attacks.
For claims on our land
they force evacuations then
destroy our homes!

Israel has been established,
on the flesh and blood
of innocent Palestinians.
Palestine is not a fictitious action film,
full of terror and killing scenes,
Palestine is not Israel,
and Israel is the occupied Palestine.

10 – PALESTINE IS RAPED

She was a beautiful lady,
with pitch black eyes and porcelain skin.
She used to get up early,
jump on the bus and travel to school.
The bus was always crowded with
different nationalities of people.
You could call it:
"The Bus of the Globe"

Palestine is a very polite girl.
She sits near the window,
after saying " Good Morning"
with a big smile on her face.

Day after day throughout the years,
a lot of strangers traveled on the bus,
from different countries.
But these new visitors
spoke Hebrew.
They used to sit together,
and make trouble all the time.
They started to bully her,
as she was quietly sat
watching the world go by.
She was a fragile girl,
and the other nations knew
about this on the bus.

But they just watched on in confusion.

She complained to the bus driver,
as she feared for her life.
These Hebrew speaking people showing her
weapons and knives.
Unfortunately the bus driver,
who carried them all,
was part of the bullying ring
to kick her out and take her place.
So he said not a word back to her,
and only encouraged them more,
so the bullying increased.

She went to tell her family members,
but found them to be not listening.
It was the bus driver who was in control,
to her horror she realized
that this was no
ordinary bus driver, but the driver
of the globe!
It represents the great power of the time.
They were all against Palestine,
as they said, at the time "she has no relatives".
She cannot fight back.

One day the bus driver decided to gather
his people to rape Palestine.
They took her seat,
kicking her out of the bus,
they called her seat "Israel"!
There after they started their killing
spree and destruction.
Attacking to remove Palestine's name
from the global bus.
They tried to deceive the world with
lies and misinformation,
but the truth STILL remains.
Palestine was here and will always stay
for all those that knew her
and will remain in their hearts.

11 – I LOVE YOU

People love their beloved,
when they are teenagers,
but I loved you.
When I was a little child,
the moment I inhaled
my first breath of your air.

People gain love,
by their relationships with each other,
but my love is innate,
or you could say it is
inherited from my forefathers.
My love is not for lust,
it is a sincere love,
from the depth of my heart.

The lovers will not be able
to comprehend this love for you,
because it's a different type of love.
Lovers love each other with human intimacy,
but I love my homeland in blood
running through my very veins
and this love is eternal.
With crises and troubles the love between
lovers can be destroyed,
but this love is unique.

The crises and trouble only increased
my tie to you.

Oh the crises we faced.
Nearly seventy years of
torture and killings.
Hundreds of thousands of lives lost
Over the years.
The pain and suffering,
genocide and atrocities over and over,
the human bodies were piling,
but it just increased my love to you.
If you were hell,
I would still feel it paradise.

The one who lost gold,
in a market of gold,
will find it again.
And the one who lost a beloved,
after a time can find another.
But the one who lost a homeland,
where can you find that?
If you search for a homeland like mine,
i am not sure it will be like Palestine.
I love you, Palestine.

12 – PALESTINE AND THE JUDGE

Hey you there ......,
what's your name?!

I quietly replied
It's me, Palestine,

You always make trouble,
and you have a terrible record,
we're fed up with all the problems.
You attack the Israelis,
and create chaos in the land.
What do you have today? They asked.

Pardon me, my judge,
I will start my story from the beginning.
I was born a long time ago,
and my mother called me Palestine.
My pain and misery started nearly
seventy years ago,
when the strangers came to me.
They raped my land, then tortured,
and forced my people to leave
their homes and farms.

They threatened us with weapons,
which were given to them,
by the big bosses in the west.

They stole our possessions and wealth,
they will not leave us alone.
They started killing my men,
women, and children.
They even follow us to the refugee camps,
to kill and commit atrocities there
against the innocent Palestinians.

They occupied my cities and villages,
deprived us from my holy places,
and removed my inheritance,
to prove that it is their land.

They killed thousands of martyrs.
All my sons are wounded,
I have a lot of orphans and widows,
they demolished my homes,
and attacked hospitals and schools.
They put my sons and daughters in prisons,
because they defended my land.
They used all prohibited weapons,
toward my people.

Now, my Judge,
you can judge for justice,
and I trust your judgment.
I will ask you now,
Am I the victim,
and are they my oppressors?

Listen, Palestine,
I don't have a choice,
I understand your frustrating cause.
The world knows too,
that Israeli stole your land,
and they are responsible for,
all the killings and violations.
But I cannot publicly declare
you are the victim,
As I myself will be in danger.

Listen, Palestine,
no one will be able to bring,

REAL justice for you.
Unfortunately we are
all so indoctrinated
to achieve the interests
of the powers that be.
They are nearly all controlled by Israel.

Don't believe in human rights,
the international security council,
and even the united nations,
they are all too weak,
against the elite.
Their purpose is to serve the leaders now,
while publicly showing democracy.

Go home and be patient,
You must endure
this pain and suffering,
till our world wakes up.

13 – FROM UNDER THE RUBBLE

You have different experiences,
from the people of Gaza.
Nothing will break them.
You have attacked them several times.
Killed thousands of innocents,
burned hundreds of children,
killed our mothers and fathers,
demolished thousands of homes,
made a lot of people homeless.
Many people say,
"if the force does not end you,
it strengthens you"

So many years of killing sieges,
lack of power and water,
and limitless obstacles and troubles,
to kill the will of my people.
But you and others will never
be able to kill it,
because it is not something
you can just take from us easily.
For you should all know by now,
our mother's milk given to us from birth,
only strengthens the love for our land.

You used all kinds of weapons,
to kill my beloved country men.
You caused thousands of martyrs,

hundreds of thousands more were wounded.
Widows are in each home,
and orphans created.

You put heaviness in our hearts.
You are the reason for all of our loss.
You ripped parts of our bodies
so they are spread out on the roads,
you slaughtered us without mercy.

You are nothing less than butchers,
who love to feast on the sight
of human flesh.
It is the flesh and blood of innocents.
You forced our parents to leave,
their beautiful, ancestral land.

I would like to say to you,
you can kill as much as you like.
Burn all our children,
destroy every Palestinian home.
Cut us into pieces,
use all your power,
and your weapons.
Use all what you will,
but you will not break us,
we will not bow down to you.

We will heal the wounds,
and honor the martyrs.
We will bury our children,
and hug our orphans.
We will get out from under the rubble,
stronger than before,
'til our will strengthens,
and it shall once more.

14 – THE HOMELAND

My son, I know you feel fed up here
you want to discover a future.
You look for peace and freedom,
with no siege or crises every day.
You have many high aims to achieve,
and you look for a better way.
I am sure, there is no lack of power within.
Here there is lack of water and gas.
I know you are also afraid of loss,
you feel if you leave
all of your loved ones will pass.

But I have some words to say
my son, please keep them
as a ring in your ear.
It will be so beautiful out there.
you will live peacefully,
without killings or bombings,
and you can raise your children without fear,
no more massive sounds of rockets.

My son there,
you will drive a nice car.
you will meet a beautiful wife,
Everything will be available,
you won't worry for water or gas.
There will be no siege like over here,
no more wars like you see in Gaza.
You will not hear the sounds of explosions.

You will not be afraid anymore for
your wife or your children.
You will not see parts of bodies
strewn on the streets.
Instead there will be flowers and
roses beside the streets.
You will see planes flying over,
don't be afraid,
these planes are only for peaceful rides.
They don't look like the ones in Gaza,
which launch rockets and bombs.
You will stay in your home,
without calls to evacuate.
You will not see demolished
homes over there from bombs.
There will only be lush greens
and beautiful homes.

My son,
you will find the paradise there,
but that paradise I know will never be
enough to satisfy your dream.
It will not be able to compensate you,
for your homeland.
You will miss the air in Gaza,
and the loving people here.

You will still feel a stranger,
even with all the years you spend there,
and the days will prove you that.
You will miss the soil of Gaza,
which can never be forgotten,
and you will discover that the homeland
is the one and only paradise.

15 – OUR GREAT SIN

We will be patient,
we will present our bodies, our children,
our very souls as gifts to this homeland.

We will fight fiercely,
'til the last blood drops,
and the last breath is inhaled.

We will endure all obstacles,
to show the world our patience,
we will never be eradicated.
As you know my friends,
when you cut the branches of a tree
it does not bend,
it will not die.
Kill as much as you can,
destroy our homes,
and commit atrocities.
We will never give up,
our branches have gone,
But more will grow.
We still have very long roots,
which go deep into our ground,
They extend everywhere,
They can never be eliminated.

The sadness and tears,

flooded to our roots.
The branches will sprout leaves of hope,
to share with its past,
of all the martyrs, the wounded,
the orphans, the widows and the homeless.
Nearly seventy years of killings,
atrocities, genocides, and collective punishments.

Have so many years not been enough,
to wake up humanity?
To tell the truth.
Palestinians are dying without mercy,
from their brothers and enemies alike.

What is our great sin I ask you?,
Even Adam and Eve were forgiven,
But we are still waiting for
forgiveness,
from the one-eyed world.
The world of Satan,
the world of injustice,
and your so-called democracy.

We did no major sin.
Mary did no sin to have Jesus,
Yet he was persecuted.
and now our great sin?
It is just that we are Palestinian.
we were born to Palestinian parents,
Who fed us only dignity.

16 – HOPELESS FACES

When you look at us,
you will recognize,
the meaning of tiredness.
The meaning of loss and hopelessness.
The meaning of refuge and homelessness.

We are the hopeless faces,
but remember, we are not one,
we are the face of millions.
I am just one of the faces
of a father who lost his son.
My heart is still bleeding,
and the sadness doesn't go.
Every day and every night I remember,
you come into my mind,
although you live in my heart.
I remember the hour of your death,
I wait for the knock on the door,
That distinct smell that
only belongs to you,
still comes out from within your room,
it wakes me up in the night.
I take your blanket in my hands,
It's cold, I need to cover you,
but when I look, your bed is empty.
I keep your blanket ready there,
with hope you find your bed once more.

Even though I know,
the dead will never come alive,
I cannot help but ,
deceive my heart.
I tell myself you will come back
only if it's just for tonight.

I am the face of the mother,
who found her baby killed.
In a soft and little crib,
I remember the scene as if
it happened today.
The shrapnel flew and shattered the room,
it hit you so fast.
All I remember now was the blood.
I fainted and woke up in a daze.
Where's my baby I kept calling,
I felt my breasts heavy
as the milk poured out,
it was mixing with the blood.
I could not comprehend
you are gone.
Now I cuddle your toys,
it still has some of your blood,
I cannot wash it out.
I refuse to wipe you out.
"You will always reside in my heart"
I say in a silent shout

I am the face of a widow,
they killed my husband,
during a dark night.
He went out to buy medicine I remember,
for our little child,
who was burning up with fever.
As we waited 'til morning
for him to come back,
I finally opened our door,
only to find my beloved.
Lying on the street below,
as a martyr he bled
until he reached our home.
but he managed no more,

his soul left his body before he could see us.

I am the face of a homeless guy,
bring me a red pencil and I will draw for you.
I will draw the images
of the many planes hovering above,
and the rockets falling.
My home was destroyed,
I will paint the house red,
I know it's a little strange,
but it will mean a lot.
I want to deliver a message,
that the dead are better than us.
At least they find tombs to live in,
but we have nothing,
we are the hopeless faces.

17 – THE LONG NIGHTS

Who likes long nights?,
enjoying a cup of warm drink,
around the burning wood.
Looking at the faces of your beloved,
laughing and sharing tales,
remembering days of love,
while the candles are burning.
It gives light and hope.

But we hate the long nights,
and we hate the candles.
Nights for us are so painful and long
the heart cries from,
the severe pain,
and the mind becomes busy as
it's kept reminded of the one I have lost.
When I'm sitting,
near to the candles,
my eyes only notice the tears
falling from the candles,
it's as if they can feel my pain,
and they are also crying for me,
showing me their sympathy
they cry and they cry.
I feel they miss my beloved as well,
they miss the sound of
our voices together.

The place is so silent now,
and the walls are waning,
unable to see the shadow of my beloved one.
I used to see her every night,
we would be chatting till the dawn.

the rain distorts
your image from the wall,
and the wind blows out the candles.
Shall I try touch your image on the wall?
or shall I close my eyes to see you
in my dreams?
I smell your body,
i reach for your pillow,
putting my face against its softness,
to feel the silkiness of your hair,
and touch your beautiful skin.

I hate winter and its long nights,
it opens up closed stories,
just to re-live all the sadness,
and refresh the pain inside.

18 – WHERE SHALL I START?

My words become lost,
where shall I start?
My tongue is unable to express,
the miserable life in Gaza.
My fingers are restricted,
they are not able to write.
The cold weather has frozen them,
and the darkness covers my mind,
it is unable to light up thoughts.
The eccentric mood,
destroys my volition to start.

Shall I start with
the young martyr,
the one who lost his innocent soul,
because of the missiles,
the little one was torn,
his body parts were later
gathered up to identify.

Or shall I start with,
a brother who was killed by the settlers.
They stole his life for no reason.
I have now been left to care
for the wife and his children.

Or I could start with a home,

which was attacked during the night,
while winter is attacking.
The homeless and bare children were shaking.
they were shivering
in the bitter cold night.

Maybe I'll start from,
the siege which was imposed,
Many years ago.
So many years of siege,
will kill all aspects of life.
No way to leave,
your studying becomes useless.
Dying here is better than waiting,
there at the gate of our brothers
in the south,
all doors are closed toward us,
except the door of God
which will never be closed.

I will start from,
the lack of power.
Six hours a day are not enough
to bake your bread,
boil water or to have a shower.

Please, remember the list
of the things we are denied,
we have lack of fuel,
A lack of water,
A lack of work,
A the lack of gas,
A the lack of food,
And a lack of precious o life.

The ones who were killed,
seem the lucky ones now.
No more pain or suffering,
no more shame in living like an inmate.
We also sometimes start to wish,
under the earth might be better,
rather than on its surface
We are the walking dead,

whose souls have been killed.
Our dead bodies still walk,
awaiting the rockets to die.

19 – PLEASE LISTEN WHEN WE TELL YOU

Please, listen.
You have been silent for a very long time
You pretend of democracy,
sing about freedom,
and announce rights for humanity.
Build organizations and councils,
to defend such principles.

Please listen when we tell you,
you destroy humanity,
by your injustice and laws.
You support the murderer,
blame the victim,
and attempt to spread freedom.
So please come to Gaza
and take a good look.
Support us to get our freedom,
or don't we belong to the human race?
Animals have rights,
are we less than that?
Why are we not
mentioned on your agenda?

Please listen.
We are the Palestinians,
we live in the Middle East,
we are oppressed by Evil,

who can only exist on our land.
They demolish our homes,
kill our children and women,
commits genocide and atrocities,
against the innocent civilians.
Sixty years of occupation,
is this called democracy
or it is called modern freedom?

Please listen.
The whole world hears,
about a rusty old rocket falling on Israel,
an Israeli soldier was killed,
a settler was hit by a stones,
a western dog was injured,
a Muslim killed a cat,
while we are dying every moment,
by your weapons and soldiers,
thousands of martyrs,
hundreds of thousands injured,
limitless numbers of orphans,
and thousands of widows,
who lost their lives,
with your taxes.

Please listen,
we witness the latest aggression,
in your fake world,
we are the oppressed,
by your oppression.
We lost our land,
our loved one, our relatives,
we are the owners of this land,
This is Palestine, not Israel.

Please listen,
you steal our freedom,
with your false principles.
You take our lives,
by your fabricated democracy,
which was only made for your people,
But not for us.
Is it made to serve only your interests?

I thought it is justice to serve all.

Please, it is time to speak loudly,
after your long silence.
It is time to tell the truth,
after all the false news
which deceived the world.
Please, will you start now?

20 – A MESSAGE TO THE SEA

I love you as you are,
I adore your breeze in the morning,
and like to breathe your fresh air.
I like watching the moon,
when it reflects its beam,
on the surface of your water.
I like your rough waves in winter,
it will bring blessings.
Your strong winds
will eradicate the black hearts,
and carry our heavy sins.
I am fond of your quietness,
which gives hope and peace.

I have heard many times,
you are full of hatred,
and you are wicked,
you have no mercy in your deep heart,
which is full of monsters,
that you swallow everything,
you are the unknown,
But I adore you.
at least, when you bring your waves to Gaza,
you throw what you have inside you,
you are the only one,
who opens your gates
to the residents to leave,

you make us feel comfortable,
you erase our sadness and pain,
and purify our hearts.
You are the most merciful,
who feeds us with your blessings,
and your monsters have mercy,
more than our humans.
They have imprisoned us for years,
deprived us our freedom,
but your monsters don't.
They kill our women and children,
our monsters are more dangerous,
they drop the heavy bombs,
on the bodies of the children,
they kill the innocent carelessly.

Your heart is deep and dark,
but it doesn't make deep wounds
in our soft bodies,
and it is less dark,
than the hearts of our humanity.

We have the monsters,
who made homeless families,
and killed thousands,
we have the monsters,
who destroyed hospitals and schools,
who slaughtered children,
and tore them to pieces.

Please, take me to your deep and dark heart.
I am sure,
it is more merciful,
than our so called kind hearts.

21 – YOUSEF RAMOUNI, THE HUNG FATHER

Allahu-Akbar is loud,
tears fall,
sorrow resides in the hearts,
settlers are waiting,
in that dark place.

The mother prepares dinner,
and your children miss you,
they are waiting for you to come back,
waiting to hear the sounds,
of your beautiful bus.
They are waiting,
for toys and chocolates,
You are so late.

The mother is so busy,
calling your mobile,
there is no answer.
Bad news comes quickly,
they killed you,
inside your beautiful bus.

The nasty people,
who hate humanity,
who steal happiness,
from the eyes of your children.
They intend to make us cry non stop

and make the mother a widow.
Who have no mercy or love,
their hearts are full of hatred and dishonesty,
they killed you with your favorite tie,
they hang you inside your own bus.
Now the tie is perfumed
with the smell of your blood,
and the color changed
from pastel blue to a deep scarlet.

It witnessed their savage cruelty,
and refuses to be the tool,
but in the end the force was too strong.
It was a witness to their crime,
it came in the night,
to the minds of the killers,
while they stir in their sleep

Our father, your image is in our hearts.
We are so young,
but we will never forget you.
How can we ever forget you?
you are the mercy and compassion.
You are the love and the affection.

We are so sad for your loss,
Our hearts break,
but we survive for the Almighty says,
the martyrs are not dead,
so, please wait for us to come and join you
in heaven like here on earth, together.

Days will pass so quickly,
we will grow old soon,
and our promise to you,
will definitely come true.
Please, live in peace till that time.
This is my prayer.

22 – STOLE MY BELOVED

I don't like winter,
it always reminds me,
of the meaning of death,
of the meaning of loss.

The trees are naked,
and the sky is grey.
A feeling of depression spreads,
from the cold wind.
I wake up to my memories.
of our special times
during the long winter nights,
alone in our cage of joy,
I imagine the past.
I remember the sweet words,
and dream of my beloved wife.

You were killed by the monsters,
they distorted your lovely and innocent face.
They stole a gifted soul,
deep inside such loveliness.
They deprived me of you
during the night,
when they came with their tanks
and their cold hearts.

Shelling homes spontaneously.

Blood covered the walls,
and flesh was burnt black,
It all mixed with the sand.,
People were scared,
children were so screaming,
I could hear their cries,
in the neighboring house.
I know now
they lost their mum and dad

But it seems I am luckier,
I at least keep our only child.
Your disruptive clothes in my cupboard,
I smell them all the time,
when I pass our room.
The pain burns my heart,
when I remember your last breaths,
and your last words........
the sound stays in my head.
Now I see it's like I became deaf
after your words.
I only remember you were bleeding
down your beautiful face,
it was warm and dripped over my hands.

I remember the warmth of your blood,
when I cradled your head into my arms.
I was able to look into your eyes,
feeling your love from their depth
i wiped your tears away
along with your blood.
They separated us in this life,
and our bodies are now far apart,
but our souls are still close.
there in the sacred heaven.
We will meet again.

23 – A LAWYER IN THE COURT OF INJUSTICE"

You don't want anyone to defend you,
you can stand alone,
in their fake court.
The judge is unjust,
and the juries are servants
in their barbaric world.
They manipulate the truth
and deceive the masses,
by their wolf dressed in sheep's clothing.

They jailed your brother
and tortured him in prison.
They judged with administrative detention
to burn your heart
and kill your patriotism.
They thought you would surrender
and stop showing the world their agenda.
They used their brutalizing tortures
but they were completely delusional.

Shireen, you are the victim,
but none is worthy to defend
your cause more than yourself.
You are the ultimate lawyer,
who doesn't fear the enemy.
You stand to show the scandals
of their own crimes,

and this ugly occupation.
You defend the Palestinian rights.

You are a humanitarian and an activist
who seeks for the rights of her people.
Palestinians are humans,
who deserve to live life.

Shireen Essawi, we are all proud of you,
you are a unique woman,
you are the very essence of honor,
the synonym of dignity.
You have our deep respect.

24 – DON'T BLAME ME

Don't blame me,
I was forced to leave my land,
and left all my property there.
I left my green olive trees,
and the sweet yellow grapes.
I left everything,
except the key of my home,
and the faith that,
I will return back there one day.

Don't blame me,
I remember that day,
when they killed my parents,
and let them bleed,
under the citrus tree.
I fled away, afraid for my life,
afraid of being killed like them.

Don't blame me,
they killed my son,
during their massive attacks.
Burnt and demolished our home
over our heads.
It buried the bodies,
with debris from the crushed home.
I still remember his voice,
calling me from under the rubble,

he was crying for help,
but it was all in vain.

Don't blame me,
they turned my wife's body
into splattered parts,
when they shelled our kitchen,
with huge lethal weapons.
I carried her body in my arms,
the deep wounds
and broken bones,
in her blood soaked clothes.
I felt her soul fly to heaven,
while looking into her eyes.

Don't blame me,
when the circle of life turns,
and I have the control,
I will make all of them regret,
for the tears I shed

don't blame me,
that I'm an aggressive man.
Blame the aggressor,
who started the round.

25 – HAPPY NEW YEAR FROM GAZA

My words are broken,
my tongue is stiff.
I am so hesitant to say,
"Happy New Year",

My mind is crowded with memories,
it carries pain and tears.
All I see is suffering and miseries,
I am busy thinking about
the lost son,
found buried under the rubble.
He is now an orphan,
who misses his parents,
my thoughts are with him.

I'm thinking of the mourning widow,
and the misguided homeless,
who found their home,
Just a pile of rubble.

My body shivers looking at
these sorry children who are
without covers,
on empty tummies and
their little hearts broken.

Inside a Palestinian's body

there is feelings of great loss.
Their eyes full of tears,
as they remember their loss.

Another New Year,
as it emerges,
we are still shedding tears ,
the blood is not yet dry.
The wounds have still not healed,
our beloved are not forgotten,
and the hearts are still broken.
I will not celebrate the New Year,
while the mother is crying,
the daughter misses her parents,
the father remembers his murdered son,
the homeless are in the shelters.
Palestine has once again been raped.

All the people around the world,
will turn on the flame,
and launch the fireworks,
while homes in Gaza are dark,
because of the power cuts.
They are still burning candles,
to see each other
in the dark night,

while millions are wasted in the air,
by the owners of the fake world.
But my happy New Year will be,
the day of a free Palestine.

26 – I AM THE FETUS

I am the fetus,
who lives inside
the tight womb.
Who waits for my food
from the blood
of that sick mother,
who suffers from chronic diseases,
corruption,
wealth,
and cuffed-hands.
Who begs her necessary needs,
and works as a servant,
to the unfair world,
she serves her big bosses.

I am the fetus,
who was deformed
by the hands of my oppressors.
They want me aborted
by cutting my supplies,
in that dilapidated universe,
which is full of darkness,
and nasty guts.

I am the fetus,
who is detained,
inside a prison.

It is so narrow to move,
so dark and difficult,
and so weak to move around.
I am waiting,
to get out of that cage,
to see the light outside,
and to face these enemies.
I want to challenge them on
their freedom of speech,
and the human rights.
I am the fetus,
who's name is "Palestine".

27 – KHADER ADNIN, AN ADMINISTRATIVE PRISONER

My name is Khader Adnan,
a Palestinian prisoner in the Israeli jail.
I'm an administrative prisoner,
with an unlimited sentence.
My residence is the solitary cell,
inside the dark and nasty jail.
My nationality is a Palestinian,
under the Israeli occupation.

They have arrested me for the eighth time.
I faced all kinds of torture,
beating, isolation, and bad treatment.
My accusation is just for being a Palestinian,
Who defends the legal rights,
and seeks for restoring back the stolen lands,
from the thieves of Palestine.

I will never give up.
If they killed me,
or they destroyed my body's parts.
If the salt eats my body,
or the chains cut my hands.
If my eyes lose their vision,
or my feet refuse carry me.

I will start hunger strikes,
One after the other,

till they surrender to my will,
of getting my freedom.
I am ready to die
for the sake of my Palestine.
I will be an example
for the other prisoners.
I will make a school for them
and teach to NEVER give in,
a school to break the enemies arrogance,
This is now my aim.

My body is so weak and pale,
and my organs are collapsing.
I cannot raise my hands,
To even make the victory sign.
I cannot walk,
to show my captors that
I am still strong,
but it is enough
to confirm though that
my freedom is more precious
than their food.

28 – LOOKING FOR CRUMBS

The wind blows strongly,
the cloud hovers highly,
the rain showers heavily,
and the darkness is spread completely.

He is living under the rubble
of a once beautiful home,
which was destroyed by Israel.
The home came down,
over the heads of all the family,
the taste of death came knocking on his door.
With that he lost his entire family.
The exception was his beloved mom,
who survived but unable to walk

He is only twelve years old,
but takes care of his injured mom.
Collects woods and dead branches,
to make the cave warm.
In order to alleviate
the pain of his mother,
he cooks and feeds her
with his own little hands.
Only for him there is nothing left,
except the empty pan.

He is looking for crumbs,

for something to eat
inside the derelict home.
He also searches for another thing,
he hopes to find humanity,
but he suspects that died
many years ago.

29 – MY DARK ROOM

Sometimes, I need to be alone,
get some rest,
and think effectively,
I close my eyes,
and dream of butterflies.
Think of the color of the sky,
over the streets of my town.
The sunbeams come through my window,
bringing light and warmth
to my dark room,
It was burnt with the fire of a bomb,
the color black now covers my wall,
It only reflects the ugly face,
of the oppressors,
who burn the children,
And kill all of the angels.
The burns on my pillow,
only confirms the terror
I witnessed in my room,
which I relive every night.
With every blink of my eyes,
I see the missile coming,
to burn me in my room.

I await the absent sun
to come and light,
my dark room.

It misses the light,
from this dark world.

30 – SANTA OF GAZA

You spread love,
peace and happiness.
You wear your beautiful suit,
and children await you,
with happiness and anticipation.
The children like the tree,
which is full of lights,
and inspires them with hope,

Santa,
don't you want come here too,
to spread of your kindness,
and show the little ones love and hope?
But it seems to me that,
you will not be able to come.
i do not blame you- in fact,
I excuse you from my heart.
I know Gaza is closed from normal life.
They closed all of our borders,
we are in a huge prison as you know.
But you can come with a boat,
through our sea,
but please be careful,
because they will kill you.
and change the blue water to red,
with not just your red suit but with your blood too,
they have no mercy for the children of Gaza,

their Talmud teaches them we are goyim.
We are not human.

Santa,
my small town needs you,
and all the children await you,
but there are a lot of children,
that are so afraid of your red suit,
it reminds them of blood,
from massacres they encountered,
on their mothers, their fathers,
their brothers and their sister.
You will remind mothers,
of their children,
who were murdered.
With lots of parents and children gone
who will bring them presents?
You will remind the children too,
of their toys buried under the rubble.
Santa, Please don't come to Gaza.
You will bring tears to the eyes,
and fresh sadness in the hearts.

Santa,
I will put the Christmas tree,
over the rubble of the homes.
I will light up the place,
and give hope and joy,
in spite of this miserable life
in spite of broken hearts.
The tearful eyes.
The lost love.
It will change the atmosphere,
of sadness and sorrow,
to an atmosphere of love and peace.
I will let people in all the big cities
see the lights from Gaza.
To tell the world that,
we are still alive,
and we will never be broken.

31 – SHIREEN ESSAWI

The mothers give birth to daughters,
and Palestine delivered you.
You are so special,
like the complete moon in the dark night,
and the glamorous star in the pure sky.

You are the symbol of freedom,
and you are the best of heroines.
You are strong enough,
to defeat your enemies.
You are stronger than their chains,
and the bars will fall down
in front of your feet.
Your big smile like the bullets,
which kill your jailers,.
They will never be able,
to make it disappear.

You are a Palestinian lioness,
who will chase the cowards,
who seek to break down your will.
They don't know that,
you are like the stubborn mountain,
that none can ever move.
But it can throw its lava,
to burn their hearts inside the bodies,
you will be their ghost,

which will attack their dreams,
and turn it to nightmares.

The ironic bars will collapse
the heavy chains will be broken,
the closed gates will be opened.
The dark nights in the detention,
will be so light.
The beams of freedom
will touch your body,
and the deep breaths of the Palestinians,
will heal all your pain and suffering.

32 – THE BANDITS

They are all bandits,
Aren't they?
They came to us as gangs.
Commit crimes and massacres,
against an innocent land.

They are bandits,
Aren't they?
They have stolen Palestine,
and fired the Palestinians.
They cut the olive trees,
and demolish our homes.
They devastated the mosques and churches,
and split up cities and villages.

They are the bandits,
Aren't they?
They kill our children,
and sever them into parts.
They blow up the homes,
over the residing population.
They made our mothers cry,
ladies lost their husbands.
They burnt so many innocent bodies,
with their massive bombs.

They are the bandits,
Aren't they?
They spread around terror.
and frighten the children.
Use prohibited weapons,
run over the citizens,
and burn the fields.
They are the bandits,
Aren't they?

33 – THE PIGEONS AND THE CROW

They have lived in peace and safety,
and have flown near and far.
They have enjoyed living in the cottage,
and they ate the seeds and the crumbs.

The crow was flying,
looking for innocents and blood.
He was lost there,
and he was searching for the carcasses.
He envied all the pigeons.
While hovering over their homes,
he noticed the prosperous life and welfare.
He came around the cottage,
examined the surroundings,
and he plotted the machinations.

He prepared a plan,
to attack the pigeons.
He started with the chicks and eggs.
He became the nightmare in the night,
and he became a reality during the day.

He called all the crows,
with his loud sound,
to settle on the cottage,
and kick the pigeons out.

The pigeons appealed to other birds,
but none wanted to help,
Even though it's an injustice by law,
it was still imposed by the powers that be.
The crows went ahead with their slaughtering and devastation.
a dead pigeon here another wounded over there.
Their blood was dripped on the white sand turning it crimson.
The rest of the pigeons flew into the open sky,
but they awaited their return someday with peace,
that would once again settle on their cottage,
and justice would reside in Palestine once more.

34 – THE WHITE VISITOR

You start the year,
with your white snow.
It's white color refers
to the purity and optimism,
with hope to bring
peace, love,
warmth and stability.

You have come as a guest.
You are a quick visitor,
bringing presents and gifts,
and most importantly,
you cover the land,
with your bright snow.
It buries the miseries and suffering,
erases the red blood,
that was mixed with the sand.
It hides the shredded bodies,
over the Palestinian land,
which witnessed the crimes.
Removes the fragrant scent
of the beloved ones,
because of your frozen air.
It heals the broken hearts
with white bandage.

You are so beautiful,

when you snow
Covering the branches of olives,
and turning the Yellow dome
into a bright white.
I know your white heart is so
compassionate and sympathetic.
Especially to the homeless,
who seek shelter in the tents,
making your snow,
as their cozy scene,
with lots of lit candles,
please, keep them warm.

35 – TWENTY OR TWO THOUSAND

All the media outlets announced:
"Breaking News"
The red headlines on all the channels,
became very alarming.
The internet was crowded,
with Charlie Hebdo's name.
And then all the leaders
showed true hypocrisy,
they condemned the terrorism.
Horrified of such an action
against their biased human rights.

All the world leaders
protested on the Paris streets,
showing their faithful condolence.
They all unite against terrorism,
which was created by them
to deceive the people,
and achieve their interests.

Twenty were killed,
shock and horror was so furiously spread.
Like Niagara falls, it was gushing down with chills
at all the political and human levels.
So when two thousand and more
were killed by one of the participants,

are they too not worthy to be announced?
The media we see so often
manipulates the truth,
but for the ones that know, I ask you
are they not enough to protest for?,
Do they not deserve the world leaders
to come to the Gaza streets
and unite against the terrorists?,
it's a real shame,
to see the killer in that
for the victim's funeral,
demanding justice for the dead.

Two thousand,
have the same souls and bodies,
like the twenty who allegedly died.
Believe me
they too were humans,
but it seems that
the twenty are only humans,
because they are from the west,
while the two thousand
are forgotten
because they are Palestinians.

I quit from such a world,
and for sure,
from the humanity,
because it is for people who are all the same,
but I will never quit,
from being a Palestinian.

36 – WRATHFUL WARRIOR

Your ugly sky,
which brings my depression,
especially, your grey clouds.
The sounds of winds,
which whistle through the rubble,
vow the unexpected storm,
and the sands fly on the faces,
to make them waning and pale.
The severe cold chases
the bare bodies,
without heavy clothes.
The broken hearts,
who have enough of the pain,
and sufficient suffering.
The pain of their beloved loss,
and the suffering of the rest.
The fractured bones of bodies,
which knock the nerve of the best.
Then you come wrathfully,
bring the cold weather,
the strong winds,
the heavy rain.

You have prepared yourself well,
and have brought all your soldiers
to attack our naked bodies,
our fragile children,

our weak tents,
and hungry families.

It seems you don't know me,
I am the orphaned Gaza,
I am the broken heart,
and I am the besieged city,
isn't that enough for you,
to show some mercy,
upon the homeless,
who has nothing except a tent,
which will not protect them,
from your cats and dogs,
and upon the poor,
who has nothing to eat,
or warm his frozen body?
you are really a wrathful winter.

"Robbie's poetry"

Hearing the rain against the tin of the roof,
I think of the pain, how my arms have got so thin,
The pain is like pins,
And in the air words full of sin,
Mis-justice and pain is the norm,
Like the rain before a storm,
My life being effected,
My family's pride rejected,

We lost our house, our possessions and our freedom,
Our misery is in full reign, our minds full of anguish,
Misjudgment and injustice flooding in our lives,
And holding us prisoners in a room full of thorns,
Our situation is not a memory,
But something we live in,
Day after day our hope is crushed,
Like gold dust thrown in the rubble,
Our lives just a muddle,

Our fate is not ours to keep,
Instead it is crushed like flowers,
In the angry palms of those who hate,
Our hopes are precious,
But are thrown to the desert,
They hit the ground like blood,
Drawn from the hands of thugs,
Noises like thunder rumble,
Innocence lost every second as we stumble,
What can we do but,
Watch all of this beauty crumble.

Written by Robbie Hoque

ABOUT THE AUTHOR

Ahmed A. Miqdad

- ❖ A Palestinian poet born in 1985
- ❖ A resident of Gaza, Palestine
- ❖ Married with three children
- ❖ Has a bachelor in English language (BA)
- ❖ Has a master in Education (M.Ed)
- ❖ Has witnessed over 3 wars and sever aggression by Israeli forces on the Palestine people since the 1980's. With a huge loss of life
- ❖ Published two previous books of poetry. First one "*Gaza Narrates Poetry*" and a second one called "*When Hope Is Not Enough*"